# I AM WOMAN
## Defining Womanhood and Identity

Dr. Camesha Hill-Carter
Editor-in-Chief

Copyright © 2017 4123 Press Publishing

All rights reserved.

ISBN-10:0972945059
ISBN-13:978-0972945059

## DEDICATION

This book is written to every unsung hero that makes a difference in this world; in the shape and gender of a woman. She is the backbone of the world and she is in control. This is written for you Queen! This is written for you too princess because our [woman] story is untold. You will face astronomical and atrocious circumstances but your will survive; whether the situation is by someone else or self-inflicted – YOU WILL SURVIVE and OVERCOME!
This is for you!

# CONTENTS

| | |
|---|---|
| Acknowledgments | i |
| The Beginning | ii |
| Belief In the Divine | 14 |
| Understanding Your Worth | 17 |
| Identity | 26 |
| Strength | 32 |
| Endurance | 44 |
| Resilience | 50 |
| Bravery | 61 |
| Overcoming | 71 |
| Miracles | 79 |
| Rebirth | 82 |
| About the Authors | 89 |

# ACKNOWLEDGMENTS

Where do I begin? I would like to thank the following people: Tonya Wilson, Candice Cox, Dr. Froswa Booker Drew, Dr. Monique Maxey, Dr. Shonta Smith, Evangelist Kelly L. King, Queen Leia Lewis and Kimberley Jones for being featured authors. I want to thank and introduce Andrea Stumon, Donna Troy, Mother Ida Jefferson, Mother Vanessa Sutton, Dawn Warren and Wendy Winegardener for selflessly giving of your story and yourself.

I want to especially thank the Facebook Team who post and encourage the I AM Woman: Defining Womanhood and Identity- Thank you Pamela Sampson, Linda Terrell, Lisa Midgett, Sherry McKie , Kenyatta Sampson, Lavenia Harris, Kenyatta Woods, Sonja Lester, Brenda Hargrove and Courtney Moses.

T. Estacia White!!!! I would not have done this without you! Thank you! Thank you! Thank you!

To all my dream partners and sounding boards, I thank you too.

*Dr. Camesha Hill-Carter, et. al*

# THE BEGINNING

# AIN'T I A WOMAN?
## by
## Sojourner Truth

## Delivered 1851 at the Women's Convention in Akron, Ohio

Well, children, where there is so much racket there must be something out of kilter. I think that 'twixt the negroes of the South and the women at the North, all talking about rights, the white men will be in a fix pretty soon. But what's all this here talking about?

That man over there says that women need to be helped into carriages, and lifted over ditches, and to have the best place everywhere. Nobody ever helps me into carriages, or over mud-puddles, or gives me any best place! And ain't I a woman? Look at me! Look at my arm! I have ploughed and planted, and gathered into barns, and no man could head me! And ain't I a woman? I could work as much and eat as much as a man - when I could get it - and bear the lash as well! And ain't I a woman? I have borne thirteen children, and seen most all sold off to slavery, and when I cried out with my mother's grief, none but Jesus heard me! And ain't I a woman?

Then they talk about this thing in the head; what's this they call it? [member of audience whispers, "intellect"] That's it, honey. What's that got to do with women's rights or negroes' rights? If my cup won't hold but a pint, and yours holds a quart, wouldn't you be mean not to let me have my little half measure full?

Then that little man in black there, he says women can't have as much rights as men, 'cause Christ wasn't a woman! Where did your Christ come from?

*Dr. Camesha Hill-Carter, et. al*

Where did your Christ come from? From God and a woman! Man had nothing to do with Him.

If the first woman God ever made was strong enough to turn the world upside down all alone, these women together ought to be able to turn it back , and get it right side up again! And now they is asking to do it, the men better let them.

Obliged to you for hearing me, and now old Sojourner ain't got nothing more to say.

## *Introduction*

"Ain't I a Woman" extemporaneously rang out in the Akron Ohio Women's Conference in 1851. Born into slavery as Isabel Humphreys but soon took on the pseudonym of Sojourner Truth, as she proclaims the Gospel of Truth, "Ain't I a Woman?", yes. "Ain't I a Woman?", Yes. "Ain't I a Woman?" YES! Yes, I am a woman. I am a woman that stand on the shoulders of slaves of Somerset Plantation in, Virginia and the lands of Mississippi. I am the daughter of Avis, who challenged her girls to exceed status quo and become phenomenal. I am a woman whose literary mind was shaped by Nikki Giovanni, Sonia Sanchez, Terri Mc Millian, Bebe Moore Campbell, Gwendolyn Brooks, Toni Morrison, Dr. Maya Angelou and others who are too numerous to name but are essential to the wit and will of the person I call woman.

Dr. Angela Davis, Shirley Chisholm, Dorothy I. Height Patricia Mitchell Bowman and Dr. Mary McLeod Bethune illustrated educational prowess that in all things attained. These women knew that the pen is mightier than the sword and changing policy to change lives is the hallmark of effective change. Using their brilliancy to usher a generation of women into education and articulation of thought for things that were not comparable to the human mindset; they stood in the gap for women's rights then as we stand for women's rights now.

Serita Jakes, Glenda Cole, Victoria Osteen, Connie Cahill, Dr. Juanita Bynum, Lisa Bevere, Dr. Cindy Trimm, Iyanla Vanzant and others on side of great men of God, showing women how ministry and marriage goes hand and hand. Even through their individualism, those without a mate, have conquered

I AM WOMAN: Defining Womanhood and Identity

the stereotypical constructs of the world and raised the standards for all to follow.

Marcia L. Fudge, Loretta Lynch, Hillary Clinton, Carrie Meeks, Maxine Waters, and Oprah all stood up, showed up and spoke up for the needs of all . There are many countless others that have held the blood stained banner for the rights of all, especially women.

Also, I must pay homage to those who are unsung or invisible- the woman and slaves, who have been second and third class citizens.

However, even in the twenty-first century women are not on the equal footing with their Caucasian male counterparts. Even today, women make $0.12 less than Caucasian men and African American women making even less according to the Women's Bureau of the Department of Labor[1].

Where does that leave us? Does that leave us at the end of the row where women are still not accounted? Do we continue not to have an identity? Are we not women? Who is going to tell our story, that we, as women, still have people who believe that women should be barefoot and pregnant in order to receive services for health care and nourishment; jobs and equal rights and standard shelter and the spirit of a humanistic being.

Currently, women are fighting for pre- existing conditions that directly affect the life and livelihood of women and women's health. Some of the issues are not being able to have the right to have birth control, cancer treatments, and treatments for other deadly conditions that can be caught or cured through preventive care. What is so sad, these same misogynistic egotistical people are the same ones who

I AM WOMAN: Defining Womanhood and Identity

women do not have the exact earning potential in their respected fields. What is wrong with this picture?

In 2002, I decided to do a black history program with some young ladies, who were great speakers, who belted out Sojourner's Truth, Ain't I a Woman speech of 1851. Yes, I read the speech in high school and again in an African American Writers class, but it was not until I saw the future (the young ladies that performed the speech) that I began to receive the fire that was given on that day to the women suffragettes, who were then, fighting for the right to vote. The speech at this particular time started a fire, a passion inside of me to see that we are truly women: women encouraged, women of love, women of passion, women of creativity, women of brilliance, women of education, women of philanthropy, women of substance, women of vision, women of worth. We are women, who are not mediocre. We are women, who are the children of the most Divine. We are women! We are women, who gives birth, creates rebirth, inspires birth. Women, whose physical identity define who they are and who they shall become through the lens of being objectified by the opposite sex. Really? Women come in a variety of colors, shapes, sizes, tones, features, personalities, and characteristics. Women, who are fair skin, brown skin, dark skin or that may have silky long hair, press, relaxed weaved, wigged or naturally curly coifs. Women, who might have round noses, round lips, round bellies, round behinds, we are women! We are still yet women, whether we wear a size 14 shoe or a size 48 in clothes. Whether we have a gap between our teeth or our teeth are perfectly aligned, we still are women! We are still women because, we are here and we have a voice now! We are women!

    We are women- hold your head up high! We are women - we cry! We are women - who can stand the brunt of turmoil and pain! We are women - represent in every facet of human life and in every arena! Yes! We are Women! Yes! We are Women! Yes, I am a woman!

4123 Press Publishing decided to begin a series of books that help identify and define womanhood. We gathered the stories of 14 women, who are at different age levels, cultures and ideas. These authors want to make a difference in the world, especially in the lives of women. These authors wrote their stories for future generations, just to let the women know, that 21st century women were not dumb or irrelevant beings or that men of that day used them as pieces of meat. We want future generations to know that women stood for life, fought on front lines of war, business, equality and peace. We want future generations to know that there were women who walked through the trenches of survival for freedoms that their children's children can enjoy. All the while we fought, we maintained our womanhood and identity; being a force to be reckoned with but being subtle, courageous, strong and loving. Women have a way of expressing their humanness like no other creature in creation. Yes, Sojourner, my global sisters and I are women!

*Dr. Camesha Hill-Carter*
*Editor-in-Chief*

## Notes

1. Based on 2013 median annual earnings of workers 15 years and older who worked full time and year-round, including the self-employed. Source: U.S. Census Bureau.

   A. Women's share of employment is based on total employed. Source: U.S. Bureau of Labor Statistics

   B. Based on 2014 median weekly earnings of full-time wage and salary workers 16 years and over, excluding the self-employed. Source: U.S. Bureau of Labor Statistics.

   C. The two highest paid and two lowest paid occupational groups or detailed occupations with at least 50,000 employed men and 50,000 employed women within these classifications.

*Dr. Camesha Hill-Carter, et. al*

## BELIEF IN THE DIVINE

## *God Created YOU In His Image*
## *by*
## *Vanessa Sutton*

God created you in his image,

So that means that you are

Special in his sight. You are

Fearfully and wonderfully made. Walk in

The dominion he has given you

On this earth. If you believe

The bible, it says that everything

God made except man, he

Spoke it into existence.

It's time for

Us to use

The power

He's given

Us

To speak

Some powerful,

Wonderful things

Into our lives.

*Dr. Camesha Hill-Carter, et. al*

Here's to the most

Magnificent life you ever

Lived through the power of

Your own spoken word. Speak

Life into every situation for

You and your loved ones.

That's the most precious gift you

Can give them. Don't be afraid

To dream outside of the box.

Take God out the little box

We put him in and let him

Live **LARGE** in you. He said you

**Can't** dream larger than He can **perform**.

He is able to do

**EXCEEDING,**

**ABUNDANTLY,**

**ABOVE ALL**

You can ask or think!!!

Now let that sink into

Your spirit and soar!!!!

God bless

## *UNDERSTANDING YOUR WORTH*

*Dr. Camesha Hill-Carter, et. al*

# "D.I.V.A."
# by
# *Authoress Tonya Wilson*

When I reflect on the question, "Describe the moment you realized that you became a woman" I automatically hear the R&B songstress, Betty Wright[1], singing in my spirit, *"Tonight is the night that you make me a woman... you said you'll be gentle with me and I hope you will... I'm nervous and trembling, waiting for you to walk in ... I've tried hard to relax but I just can't keep still... I want to play big girl and put on a sexy smile... but I know so little about what love is I just can't help acting like a child..."*

Consequently, this song, "Tonight is the Night That You Make Me a Woman" was a poem originally written by Betty Wright and as she says, *"It's the story of a young girl making love for the very first time",* and she is right because every time I hear this song on the radio, it doesn't matter how many years have passed, I'm taken back to the 16-year-old girl who became a woman on a particular night... me. I remember how nervous I was and I remember the smile on his face as he told me that it was natural and to relax. I remember, months before that encounter, my best friend who was a few years older than I, asked me why I never talk about sex and I remember how embarrassed I was to tell her that I was still a virgin and how I had changed the subject abruptly. Oh, how I wished on the night that I lost my virginity and became, "a woman" that I would have let my girlfriend give me some advice to prepare me for that special day in my life.

I AM WOMAN: Defining Womanhood and Identity

It was several decades later that I came to the realization that becoming a woman had little to do with sex and or the loss of one's virginity. Being a woman, in my opinion, is knowing your worth as one of God's greatest creations on this earth. Knowing that you were made by the hands of God as a help mate to a man that God has handpicked just for you, and knowing what the definition of a help mate really means. God said in Genesis, 2:18[2], *"It is not good that man should be alone; I will make him a help meet for him". We need to* understand that God's creation wasn't complete until He made woman. He could have made her from the dust of the ground as He did man but He decided to make her from the man's flesh and bone, and in doing so He illustrated for us that in marriage, men and woman symbolically become one in flesh. He didn't intend for the woman to slide down a stripper pole, shake her body for money, sell her body for money, or subject herself to physical, mental and verbal abuse. I'm certain that He did not mean for the woman to lead the man into sin through manipulation as Eve did to Adam in regards to taking a bite from the forbidden fruit. I wonder if our vaginas have become a forbidden fruit and if our vaginas, not money, have become the root of all evil. I would venture out to say that a man chases money but he chases the vagina even the more because even a lazy man who refuses to hold down a job and provide for his family desires sex and will go from woman to woman making deposits with his penis. The question is, "Are we fulfilling God's purpose as a woman to be a help meet to one man or are we fighting another sister over her husband? Have we lost focus of our God-given purpose as one of God's greatest creations, "Woman"?

"What it means to be a woman", in my opinion is spelled out in 4 letters, **D.I.V.A.** Yes, "Diva"!!! Be

"**Determined**" to be the best person that you can be which means respecting yourself, mind, body and soul. Be "**Dedicated**" to your destiny, your purpose and those who love you and whom you love also. Be "**Discerning**" because there are "Haters" who will want to be you and be like you. They will want to hang around to identify your weaknesses and set traps for you. Don't be eager to believe everything that you hear... use your discerning eyes and your discerning spirits.

Be "**Intelligent**" meaning to use your brains and not your body to gain popularity and prosperity. God has given woman so many gifts so become a part of the industry today and become an "**Innovator**"! Use your gifts, use your intelligence and use your hands... make something, write something, bake something, sew something, design something, craft something, draw something, paint something, and after you do all of that... "**Invest**" your money! What good is a $300 purse with not 3 cents in it? Be financially secure and bring something to the table so a man will want to sit down at your table! Don't be the woman who only brings a fork and a knife to the table. That's so unattractive! Be "**Informed**" and speak only the truth! No one like a gossiper and a liar.

My favorite is, be "**Virtuous**" and serve God. Many women today believe that being a virtuous woman only applies to the women back in the Old Testament days but my sisters, I beg your pardon. While God's Word never returns void to us, it also can stand the test of time no matter how many thousands of years passed. Being a virtuous woman doesn't mean being perfect but it means living a life with purpose, diligence, forgiveness and repentance. Study God's Word to show thyself approved. The enemy recognizes a fraud and you cannot fake the knowledge of God's Word. Remember Acts 19:15[3], "One day the evil spirit answered, Jesus I know, and Paul I know about, but who are you?" In other words, my Sisters, *"Put on the whole armor of God, that you may be able to stand against the wives of the devil. For we wrestle not against flesh and blood but against principalities against powers against the rulers of the darkness of this world, against spiritual wickedness in high places[4]."* Speak God's Word, speak life into your man and into your children, and let your home and your children be a reflection of you.

Finally, my Sisters, be "Adorable". Be adorned with God's favor, be easy to talk to and easy to listen to. Smell good, look good, be confident, walk into a room and own it, be the crown jewel in a room full of rocks and fake cubic zirconias... "Shine Bright Like a Diamond"!

In conclusion, I'm going to answer the question, "What woman do you identify with and what attributes did she give you?" I have just 2 words for you my sisters, "Michelle Obama[5]", and remember, "When they go low, we go high.

## *Notes*

1. "Tonight Is The Night", composed by Betty Wright

2, Scripture King James Version Genesis 2:18 Zondervan Publishing

3. Scripture King James Version Acts 19:15 Zondervan Publishing

4. Scripture King James Version Galatians 6:11-12 Zondervan Publishing

5. Michelle Obama's Speech to the Democratic National Convention of 2016

# I AM WOMAN: Defining Womanhood and Identity

Candice Cox, LCSW
123 Call Me Street
Any town, Anywhere, USA




To: My Broken Sista

Wherever YOU Are in Life

Anywhere USA

Right Now
Right Here
Today

My Dearest Sista,

Can I bend your ear for a second or two? As your eyes soak in these words, please let them speak to the core of you. **I don't envy you my Sista**, please don't think of me that way. I see the pain in your eyes, as your anger pushes me away. My calmness is not a sign of weakness, it's an understanding. I accept you for you.

See, you are under the impression that we are in some type of feud. No queen, not at all, I always want what's best for you! I love you, you're my sista! Loving me is loving you. Me hatin' on you is not an option. Sista, the beast you're fighting is not me boo.

If you're unhappy about your situation, please don't use me to avoid your truth. Keep healing and overcoming struggles, by realizing, admitting, and working through. You're far too precious to anchor your spirit with the demons of who hurt you. Please know, if you don't change, they will always control you.

So, no, I don't envy you my sista, I actually see great things for you. But, until you learn everything is not a battle, I'll just drop this seed in your spirit and let you do what you do.

I AM WOMAN: Defining Womanhood and Identity

Queen everyone in the world is not out to see your demise. You don't have to put on a show, to protect your porcelain pride. Be confident in your actions; don't do things without thinking them through. Because being in your feelings is one thing, but the actions behind those feelings can build or destroy you.

Let these words encourage you, boo! You don't have to remain broken ... I am here for you!

In closing, know your worth. Never let anyone lower your value. You're a Queen at all times my Sista, focus on your greatness and surround yourself with Queens striving to be great too! This is written with the utmost love and compassion.

Your Sista,

Candice

P. S. You don't have to be broken anymore.

## *IDENTITY*

I AM WOMAN: Defining Womanhood and Identity

## *It's Hard for a Black Woman*
## *by*
## *Dr. Shonta M. Smith-Love*

Oh it's Hard for a Black woman

The mother of this earth

The Queen of civilization

The teacher of every student

The one who bears life is also the one who can take that life

They take my man from me, the one I love so dearly

They take my mother from me, the one I care for so seriously

They take my God from me, the one I chose to praise

But through all these trials and tribulations

I'm like a Black cloud, roaring loud, protecting proud, striking without fear

Because at all times, I know God is near.

Fear, I don't know what that is

Pain, I go through everyday

Survival seems to be my destiny

Because Allah has chosen me to be the one who holds the key.

*Dr. Camesha Hill-Carter, et. al*

Fighting is something I do everyday

A Battle is like a Big maybe

The war is taking place now

Who will win, I say me, because I plan to go far

When will it end I ask you my friends

The journey is long, but we all must amend.

The war is not over until some die

And Black will never die because we always multiple

Oh, it's hard for a Black woman as you can see

Living in this insane world is some kind of reality

As I struggle for my existence each day

I pray to Allah to guide me the right way

But as this insane world comes to an end

It's up to you to bring out the true virtue

Because as a Black woman

A Queen I will always be

Even though it's hard in this life, I still live in this reality

Oh, it's hard for a Black woman as you can see

But who will make it easy, that one person, happens to be me.

I AM WOMAN: Defining Womanhood and Identity

## *How Can I Stop the Tears from Falling Down my Face*
## *By*
## *Vanessa Sutton*

Tell me how can I stop the tears from falling down from my face?
Tell me how can I....when I feel so much pain, shame and such disgrace?
Our children have become so insensitive, no feelings....so cold,
They shoot off at the mouth and with their elders they get very bold.

Whose fault is that, that we have let this situation get so out of hand?
Whose fault is that, that we...in "love" did not reprimand?

Whose fault is that, that we let them get this old,
Without that good old fashioned love that we got from our mothers and fathers;
Grandmothers and...grandfathers; aunts and uncles, and cousins; yes and our sisters and brothers; preachers, deacons and the old white haired church mothers?
Whose fault is that, that the traditions were not passed down and told?

The Ancients/the elders used to love the "H-E-L-L" out of us!!
They didn't leave us to our own inventions...to get into so much "STUFF"!!

Yes, they would whip our backsides and tell us when we'd done wrong,
There wadn't no cussing, fussing, and backtalk either, nor shootin' with a gun!!!

Such a thing was unheard of...talk back to the Ancients and elders...what could you've been thinking?!!
Or maybe it was that you slipped and got into the forbidden bottle and was drinking?

'Cause surely if you had been in your right mind, you'd da known betta than that.

Surely you had to have known when you sobered up and come to your senses, daddy would knock you flat on you're... a$$! ☺

NO...it wadn't no talking back and talking smack,
Cause momma and daddy wadn't having none of that!!!
The ironing cord, the extension cord, a switch, a belt, a shoe....
Anything that they could get a hold of, to beat the "H-E-L-L" out a you.

See when the "H-E-L-L" left...you had peace and rest.
And then you grew up and prospered and people called you blessed.

Blessed to have a momma and daddy that gave a damn about 'cha,
Blessed that you had a village of family folks and friends that raised and never doubted ya,
Blessed that you were not left in this world to fight alone,

I AM WOMAN: Defining Womanhood and Identity

Blessed to have that LOVE surrounding you since the day that you were born.

So...tell me how can I stop the tears from falling down from my face?
Tell me how can I....when I feel so much pain, shame and such disgrace?
How did we let our young ones of this generation slip from our grasp and not know it?
How did we let them raise themselves and the LOVE we got...we didn't show them?
How can we fix what has been broken...for oh so very long?
Let's go back to the old time way...we can LOVE and lead them home!!!

We can ask them to forgive us for leading them astray,
For not giving them the same thang, we got back in tha' day.
When the Ancients and the elders showed us how to live,
OH...and yes, most importantly, they taught us to forgive.

It's not too late, I won't believe it...no, no, no, no I won't!
We must go back and get our babies...stop per-pa-tratin...don't front!!!
We must prayerfully ask God and our children to forgive us of our sins,
Then and only then......can true inner healing begin.

Dr. Camesha Hill-Carter, et. al

## *STRENGTH*

I AM WOMAN: Defining Womanhood and Identity

## *Yes, I Am A Strong Black Woman*
## *By*
## *Ida Jefferson*

Let me tell you what I think that makes and define a woman. It is not appearance or clothing style it is the sheer ability to rise to the occasion regardless of what the situation may be.

I have seen women rise to many occasions. My greatest example is watching women achieve very demanding and arduous goals. I came to the realization that I to had come into this elicit club of womanhood at 9 years old. Yes, I was still a child but I had to learn that responsibilities made me strong and mighty in the Lord.
Through my responsibilities, I too became cognizant of how to process my behaviors and actions that would ultimately make me the woman I am today.

Throughout my life, I have conquered and attained many positions in the corporate, educational and not-for profit arenas. I held true to this thought as I now instruct others on how to be a Godly strong woman- "You are an adult. You don't have to lie." On this premise, I did not have to create shenanigans to win favor with people or to get opportunities from others. This was taught to me by many strong women and now, people will either ask my things because of my lifestyle of living in my truth or not ask me because she or he does not want my truth. Either way my example has permeated the years as I have help countless people.

Honestly, I have learned people through watching others and learning what to do and how to do it. As a woman of God, I lean on the scripture of to whom much is given much is required.[1] I remember washing 20 pairs of jeans through a ringer washer. As a young girl, the task seemed insurmountable, but learning the how with patience and understanding of others, I grew and was able to accomplish the goal. As time prevailed, I used techniques and ways to make the task even easier through observation of others and the peace of God- that surpasses all understanding[2].

You thought that was the only chore? No! My chores included preparing the Saturday and Sunday meals for my family. I had to cook two roasting pans of fried chicken, picking a huge pot of greens, peeling sweet potatoes to make two big pans of yams, big pans of corn bread and Cole slaw, by myself starting at age nine. There were no microwaves, easy cutters, or gadgets that peel and shuck any vegetable that you may have in your refrigerator.
While food was frying and baking, as the oldest, I was given the charge to clean the house and keep your brothers and sisters in line. I used my gifts and talents to train others with my brothers and sisters. I learned so much on how to deal with disgruntled employees in a kind and charismatic way.

Some time ago, I worked for a large trucking company. My second interview should have given me a clue of the climate of the company. The man conducting the interview put in feet on the desk in front of me ask if I could drive a stick shift. Of course, me being me, I said, "No! I wasn't applying for a truck driving job." I felt really bad after the interview because I let my attitude get in the way. I thought that I didn't get the position. Two days later HR called and made an offer. I counter offered because I wasn't sure how I would fair in a 90% white male environment. Knowing that God didn't bring me this far to leave me, I got the job as assistant manager in the daily rental office.

Remembering how I had started learning to be a woman at age 9, I realized that I had a lot of work to do.
On paper, I worked from 7am to 3pm. I always arrived at 6:30 to prepare for day. Due to evening person not doing their job, I had to rely on my mother wit and skills to do an exceptional job. I became fast friends with a few people. I was able to learn their techniques and make them my own.

In my second year, I had an outstanding review. I learned that the other co-worker with the same title was making $3500 more than I. This pulled on my strength in asking others to comply with the rules as I had to do so often with my brothers and sisters.

When the company did not give the raise that was comparable to my counterpart, I was leaving the company. I had built a great relationship with my immediate supervisor. He convinced me to stay. He knew of a position was becoming available in the company.

As a great friend, he did all he could to prepare me for the position of Dealer Manager. This position encompasses the entire region 125 independent dealers for places that rented trucks for local and long distances moving. The position was posted. Fear came over me. I didn't think I had any chances to really infiltrate this Old Boy's Club[3]. I put my name in the hat and started the testing process.

Two of the guys were buddies with the top guys. They seem to know things before I was informed. The current Dealer Manager gave a 90-day notice, he was relocating. Every other week, I felt like withdrawing my name. I became very stressed and started getting sick. I didn't know what was wrong with me. Three weeks before the decision, I found out I was pregnant. I told my husband and my mother I was pregnant. They both believed in me and my ability to get the position. They encouraged me to tell truth that I WAS PREGNANT and NOT withdraw my name.

"Oh boy", I cried. I knew I was not getting this position. I called my mother asking her what to do. My mother said, "Trust God, but you have to tell them". I told her that I just wanted to withdraw my name and kick rocks. My husband was very supportive as well as he encouraged me not to give up. At this point, due to my pregnancy and not knowing anyone in the top offices, I knew they will never give me the position.

I summoned up some strength and told my immediate boss. He told the General Manager. The General Manager made jokes. After that, I was defeated. I withdrew my name. I had no confidence.

God did not withhold any good thing from me[4]. To my surprise, three weeks later, they offered me the job. The power of Holy Ghost surrounded me and I got some holy boldness. I was determined not to be under paid as I was previously. My good friend who had the job coached me on what to say and do in order to get the salary I desired. I not only got the position with pay, but six months later, I gave birth to one of my three daughters.

That year, I worked very hard. Very few people believe that I was equipped or qualified for the job. I proved the all wrong. I won New Dealer of the year.

I AM WOMAN: Defining Womanhood and Identity

As a young woman, I was in training for the woman I am today. I look back over my life and have accepted the road and the lane God has for me in this season. The woman I am today comes from sacrifice, obedience, hard work and love. I come from strong women, but Ida Mae Wofford Jefferson, all by herself, is a strong woman of God!

## **Notes**

1. Scripture King James Version Luke 12:48 Zondervan Publishing

2. Scripture King James Version Philippians 4:6 Zondervan Publishing

3. A white male Southerner with an unpretentious convivial manner and conservative or intolerant attitude and a strong sense of fellowship with and loyalty to other members of his peer group. American Heritage® Dictionary of the English Language, Fifth Edition. Copyright © 2016 by Houghton Mifflin Harcourt Publishing Company. Published by Houghton Mifflin Harcourt Publishing Company. All rights reserved.

4. Scripture King James Version Psalm 84:11 Zondervan Publishing

## I ALREADY DID THAT!
## by
## Evangelist Kelly L. King MS, MA

Life is not designed to *ALWAYS* be an uphill climb, but it should be filtered with nice strolls from time to time. Too often we find ourselves living life like a Ferris wheel repeating the same mistake and living on a continuous rotation of the same problems and people. At what point do we recognize that most of our struggles in life aren't new.

When do we come face to face with issues and say hold up wait a minute "I already did that." Some of us are allowing the same things to get us hung up, whether it's fear, lack of confidence, bad relationship choices, financial bondage, complacency and on and on. At some point you have to tell yourself, your haters and our ultimate foe "I already did that", and I don't plan to do it again.

Stop allowing yourself to live beneath the life that God has predestined for you. He said, *"No good thing will he withhold from you."* Follow after that voice from the inner you that says you deserve more, and you can do more. That voice that says you are fearfully and wonderfully made. Start challenging yourself to be the best you can be.

When the enemy comes in like a flood, most times, he isn't coming with anything new. We just aren't taking the time to assess his game. Ladies, we must learn to quickly assess the situation and be armed with boldness.

We have to have the realization that we have power. Stop falling for the same ole same ole. Speak to yourself and to your situation with authority "I already did that." I don't have to be in yet another unhealthy relationship, I'm worth more than that, so if I have to wait, I'll wait.

I'm not going to settle where I am, I will pursue my dreams. I don't have to live in financial bondage hoping that I can pay my bills. I can and I will gain control over my finances, and I will make better choices. I will not be fearful because I haven't been given the spirit of fear, but of a sound mind.

Iron sharpens iron, so let me start putting myself around those that are moving forward. I will stop limiting myself because of my lack of confidence. There is more in me and I want to start living like it.

Ladies, wise up and tell your haters, the naysayers, that negative voice in your ear and our eternal foe, "I've already did that" it's time for a change up!

## **Notes**

Scriptures King James Version
Psalm 34:10
Psalm 84:11
Psalm 139:14
Proverbs 27:17
Isaiah 59:19
II Timothy 1:7
Zondervan Publishing, 2017

## Strength of Love
## by
## Donna Troy

As I have given this some thought I can identify with more than one woman. The first is my great grandmother, Elizabeth (Bessie). She greeted everyone as a human being, having something kind in each individual. Grandmother practiced everything that she read and heard about in the Bible. If she could not say anything nice about someone then she would not say anything at all. The truth be told; I am still working on this one.

Being an American Indian in the 1800's was not an easy task. However, she remained positive. This is the greatest attribute that I received from grandmother.

Richly, my grandma Letha gave me the quietness that I have about me. As a child growing up I would observe her until I became an adult. She may never have said much, she quietly sat in the room and would join a conversation every now and then. Grandma Letha had the most beautiful long gray hair. I hope that mine will look like hers one day.

My grandmother showed the love of her family through her cooking. Having step children, but you would never know it. She showed all of us how to love children even if they were not your own. I do this to this day, I think because not every child is loved and we (they) all need to know that someone cares for them.

Currently, the woman that I identify with is my mother, Mary. My mom has shown the family the true meaning of taking wedding vows until death do you part. I watched my mother do everything in her power to assist and make my dad comfortable as possible in his last days. This is a trait that I have picked up for other family members. Whatever the need, I try to assist in filling the need.

Graciously, Momma has always shown love through her cooking. I find myself fixing favorite dishes that I make for certain individuals. I make a strawberry soda cake that one of my nephews always looks for when he has a birthday or is on the honor roll. My mother and I both love to see people enjoying the food that has been prepared for the pure satisfaction that everyone is happy with the meal. I get my strength from my mother. She is one of the strongest women I know.

Being a mother of five (includes two sets of twins), she did not let anything get in the way of her children. As my father provided for the family, my mother nurtured her children.

As this is just a small portion of the women in my life, they have made me a nurturing secure, warm individual, and that has made the difference in me and in my life. I love them all for various reasons. I could not imagine their influence not being a part of my life.

## I'M STILL HERE!
### (You Can't Hold a Good Wo/Man Down)
### by
### Vanessa Sutton

When I look all around me what do I see, Darkness, death, pain and misery, Our children are dying at an alarming rate, From zero on up, going swiftly to the grave.

We are our own culprits, we eat and devour our own, Can't blame it on the white man, no not this time, It's us and us alone.

Good men out there determined to rise above it, Go to work everyday trying to make it better for their loved ones,

It gets harder and harder each and everyday, but in their hearts they believe that....God will make a way!

Why you say?

'Cause you can't hold a good wo/man down....

Now I'm 53 and I'm looking at me, And I'm asking myself do I like what I see, I'm looking at the woman in the mirror, I'm asking her to change her ways,

Why, change my ways? because if I don't change,

Everything about me will stay the same, The same ole dead tired look, the same ole tired, broke pocketbook,

My mind in a haze, for the rest of my days; That's not what the the part about me in the good Book says!

NO...I'm not going out like that!!! I'm not standing by and all my life (force) be sapped,

I AM WOMAN: Defining Womanhood and Identity

Seeping out like a leaky faucet,

Gotta make a change before death comes a calling,

Gotta make it right, make the rain stop from fallin, (On my head that is...)

Gotta get on up, gotta dust myself off, Gotta look to the Lord, 'cause

He knows it all, He's the one that can turn my life around,

Make me whole, make my mind sound. Turn it over to Jesus....Yes, that's what I'll do.

He'll work it out. He knows exactly how to. Why you say?

'Cause He said, His thoughts of me are GOOD!

He'll make everything work out just like it should.

If I acknowledge Him, He'll direct my path,

Give me more joy, and peace than I ever had!

So I'll keep on putting one foot before the other, And along the way stop and help a sista or brotha,

Lending a helping hand whenever I can, For mine eyes have seen the Glory of the coming of the Lord!

As I keep my eyes on the prize, suddenly the Sun/Son breaks through the skies, Yes...change has finally come, and I have no fear, My day looks brighter, and the sky is clear. Why you ask? 'Cause I found out...you can't hold a good wo/man down.

Thank God I'm still here,

KEEP THE FAITH!!!!

## *ENDURANCE*

## *A Realized Woman*
## *by*
## *Andrea Stumon Claiborne*

Realizing when I became a woman cannot be confined to a moment for me because I have had a series of "Aha!" moments. The first one was when I was in the third grade. As third grade students, we were told to lay our heads on our desks when we were done with our class assignments. This particular day was quite different. After completing my assignment, I folded my arms and lay my head on my desk, but "these knots" on my chest were not allowing me to do so comfortably. Although my Mom had already had "that talk" with me, I had no idea there was pain associated with blossoming and getting my first bra. (Now keep in mind that I was a third grader and imagine the level of panic and fear going through my mind.) I was so alarmed and in fear that I was dying that I informed my teacher. She tried her best to keep a straight face and informed me everything was going to be fine and she would be sending a note home to my Mom informing what we discussed. When I arrived home, Mom read the note, smiled, and said "We are just going to have to get you a bra." I was so excited!

From that moment on, so much changed in my world. I was not (exactly) what society calls a tomboy, but I easily became bored with dolls, tea parties, dress ups, and jumping rope, so I played games with the boys such as Hide & Seek, Dodge ball, Foursquare, and Curb. In addition, I would climb fences, play in the mud, and chase bees just for the sake of doing something different. Many times, I would try to play with the boys when they played football, but they always ignored me because "you are a girl" .... until one day several years later. I remember going outside one day and all of a sudden I was no longer invisible. Boys were looking, whispering, some of them giggling. At first I did not understand because I thought I was the same Andrea on that day as I was when I played Dodge ball, built mud castles, and chased bees. I remember asking my Mom "Why are they (boys) so silly?!" My Mom replied, "You are becoming a young lady." Throughout my teen years, I experienced other physically developing stages, but emotionally I did not realize I was a woman until I purchased my first car.

My very first car was a 1991 Pontiac Grand AM. When I saved enough money to purchase it, I knew two things: It had to be red (my favorite color) and I had to look good in it. Finding it and purchasing it wasn't the easiest thing at first. Initially I wanted to buy it on my own to show my independence. I went all over Shreveport looking for the perfect car. I found a few that I liked and happened to discuss pricing with some of my male family members and friends. These men burst my bubble really quickly. Why? They all said the prices were too high and I was going to get taken if I did not take an experienced car buyer (preferably a man) to help me seal my deal. I questioned how a man could negotiate better prices than a woman.

Well I soon found out because my Dad insisted on going and he was able to negotiate the same car for less than what I was offered. (I'm still pissed to this day that such a disparity exists when it comes gender, but I won't get on that soapbox today.)

To understand what makes a woman, one must first understand why the woman was created and the ingredients that make a woman. According to Genesis 2:18, "the Lord God said "It is not good that the man should be alone; I will make him a help meet for him[1]". This says man needed another version of himself to help him live well and get through life. The other version is called woman. If one was not born as a woman – no amount of physical changes makes one a woman. Being a woman is more than hairdos, fancy dresses, high heels, accessories, makeup, and emotions. As a young child, in science classes, I learned females have two "x" chromosomes and males have an "x" chromosome and a "y" chromosome. This says no matter how a man may alter his physical appearance; it will not make him a woman because he will lack the other "x" chromosome. (So when in doubt, do a DNA check! If the person lacks two "x" chromosomes, they are not a woman!)

It disturbs me that society attempts to define a woman by hair length, chest size, voice tone, color preferences, and female genitalia. The length of a woman's hair or lack of hair does not make a woman any more or any less of a woman. A bra cup does not define who a woman is. Being emotional is not exclusive to women. Singing alto/tenor does not make a woman any less of a woman than wearing pink makes a man less of a man. Surgeries definitely do not make a person a woman.

Women wear fancy, feminine hairdos. Women also wear buzz cuts. Many days we become emotional. Some of us have high pitched voices. Some of us have deep pitched voices. Some of us have the physical strength of men; others have stronger mental capabilities. We are intelligent, assertive, loving, compassionate, and sympathetic. We are thinkers, writers, inventors, teachers, engineers, doctors, lawyers, and so many other professions. We love hard. We discipline. We give birth to and bring life to so many people and ideas.

The celebrity I mostly identify with is actress Jenifer Lewis. Recently I read an article where Jenifer discussed having bipolar disorder. "Bipolar disorder is a mood disorder with distinct periods of extreme euphoria and energy (<u>mania</u>) and sadness or hopelessness (<u>depression</u>). It's also known as <u>manic depression</u> or <u>manic depressive</u> disorder[2]". Although, I do not have bipolar disorder, I have been diagnosed with Fibromyalgia. It is a very painful condition of the central nervous system. It is a condition that does not have a cure; just medicines to help deal with the symptoms. Symptoms include: migraine headaches, sensitivity to light and sound, chronic muscle pain, extreme fatigue, low energy, insomnia, and difficulty remembering. Both conditions may lead to depression or emotional distress because of hormonal imbalances or a feeling of not being well.

    I respect Jenifer Lewis because she had the courage to talk about her condition and because her personality is a lot like mine. Both of us says what is one our minds and neither of us gives a gram whether other people like it or not. We are sassy. We are strong. We are opinionated. We are intelligent. WE ARE WOMEN!

## **Notes**

1. Holy Bible. (King James version). Thomas Nelson, Inc. 2003. Genesis 2, p. 3.
2. WebMD Medical Reference. 2016. Women with Bipolar Disorder. Retrieved February 22, 2017, from http://www.webmd.com/bipolar-disorder/guide/bipolar-disorder-women#1.

## *RESILIENCE*

## Musings on Being a Girlchild, Womanhood, and Life
### by
### Froswa' Booker-Drew, PhD

> "Do not bring people in your life who weigh you down. And trust your instincts ... good relationships feel good. They feel right. They don't hurt. They're not painful. That's not just with somebody you want to marry, but it's with the friends that you choose. It's with the people you surround yourselves with."
>
> Michelle Obama

My mother, my baby girl and I always take trips out of town for Spring Break. Our girls' trips are significant not only to relax and to tour historical facilities but to bond and share memories. I always enjoy these moments because I know the value of memories and how those experiences shape who you are as a person, as a woman.

As a mother, my desire has always been to give my daughter experiences that would serve as a foundation for her future. No matter what the world will tell her about being a woman, I have been determined to make sure I tell often that she is beautiful, brilliant and powerful.

I have so many memories that have informed who I am and how I see the world today. As we drove through Arkansas and Louisiana, we had so many conversations reminding me of my past and the legacy of my family. Listening to my mother reminiscing about our family's trials and tribulations, I recognized the amount of pain, struggle and abuse the women in my family endured. I was reminded of this deep strength, faith in God, and perseverance which exists at the very core of who I am; It is wired heavily in my

DNA.

As a child, I saw the differences between women and men very early especially for Black Women. I knew my mother had a very difficult labor with me but I did not know until I was older what really happened. My mother had more than 60 stitches after my birth due to a nurse lying on her stomach to push me out. I saw the differences demonstrated in not only health care, but in the home and in church. My mother was a well-known speaker, invited to come to churches in our area to bring the welcome address or share the announcements. Men were allowed in the pulpit and my mother would have to speak in front of the pulpit at a podium. I also saw that women were treated differently in their homes. I watched women cook, serve their husbands, clean, take care of their children and even the children of others, work hard at low wage jobs, and very seldom have time for themselves. They were at the disposal of the men in the family. I watched and heard about women being cursed out and called out of their names, struck by hands and fists, cheated on and belittled for their voices and opinions.

This was a time of the past—a time that was so different than what we see today. And yet, even with all of the changes, we have in many ways, remained the same. The misogynistic behaviors that we see against women have been embedded in our media and belief system of our world today. My mother and the women in my village always pushed me to be independent, to not depend upon a man. They felt if they had an education, if they had a unique skillset, they would not be in those situations that damaged their minds, their souls, their bodies and their spirits. I found myself pushing so hard to live in the world in a way that I relied so heavily on me that the ability to ignore my needs was not that distant from the women I loved. The abuse they endured was not my abuse but the ability to endure beyond the imaginable became my story, too.

When I graduated from high school, I made a decision that I needed to get away from my home. I thought moving to a new place would change things. I could move away from the challenges I saw between my parents and others in my life. Moving was good for me, it was in that space that I found my voice when I left home. I was no longer defined by my classmates or family. I asserted my voice and ran for office the first week of school for Dorm President and won overwhelmingly. Winning that office was the continuation of my leadership journey that began in High School. Despite the success I experienced in moving into more significant opportunities in college, I found myself in relationships that were counterproductive. I dated someone who threatened suicide when I broke up with him. I had dealt with so much manipulation within the relationship—when other guys would flirt with me, I was usually accused for that happening. Despite the attempt to manipulate me to stay, I encouraged him to do what he needed to do because I would not be a part of a Jedi mind trick and that was the end.

In other relationships to follow, I recognized later that in my attempt to distant myself from men that were abusive, I actually revisited those spaces like many of the women before me. I saw and heard about the physical abuse as a child. I vowed I would not endure that in my life. Instead, I tolerated emotional abuse and neglect in boyfriends. I accepted friendships that only saw my value when I was valuable for them.

There is a theory that states those areas of our lives that are traumatic are often repeated because the mind desperately wants resolution and closure. It's not that we desire the bad things but we often draw those situations into our lives without realizing that what we seek is healing. For most of us as women, we spend so much time healing the pain of others through our professional and personal lives that the traumas that shape and frame our perspectives are left on a shelf and one day, if we don't deal with those issues, they fall unexpectedly demanding to be addressed. We are left to pick up the pieces that have not only shattered our lives but others are impacted by the collateral damage.

I'm older now and my understanding of life has broadened. It was so easy to see women as weak that would carry these unrealistic loads when I was younger. I know now that there is a remarkable strength that exists for women—to stay, to leave, to live. Zora Neale Hurston in the 1937 book, *Their Eyes Were Watching God*, referenced that black women are the 'mules of the world'. I believe that she was referencing this phenomenal strength that we all have. I am not suggesting that abuse should be tolerated or celebrated. It should not. It is the strength that should be celebrated. It is also the recognition that we need these stories to help inform, liberate, and even create communities of support.

So many of the women I saw growing up suffered in silence, hiding their pain and passions from others for fear of being once again rejected, belittled and humiliated for thinking, having a vision or standing up for themselves. I realized from my childhood that many women forgo their dreams, their happiness at the expense of others. It is amazing that as you enter the fourth decade of your life that you experience a euphoric awakening....that carrying the loads of others could be a point of reference but it does not have to become the additional baggage needed for the life journey.

As a child, I saw women who did not have many relationships with other women. We were told to keep our business as our business. Those who had access to our lives were limited because it was important to keep up the façade. I saw women who came to church on Sunday dressed out of sight, falling out in the church because of the spirit and always had a Scripture to speak for others. Many of those women were going home, removing the mask of perfection and holiness to change into a new outfit—the complete opposite of their performance---to shame, guilt, insecurity, anger, resentment and disappointment. They did not share with others what they were going through and I learned very young that women could not be trusted. We were competing for attention, recognition, and love. This belief system eliminated any possibility for support until it was often too late. As a teen, I adopted this viewpoint and very seldom allowed myself to get close to other girls because they would hurt me and disappoint me. I was bullied in elementary school by several girls and this further enforced my view. I had a few girlfriends from middle and high school that remain my dear friends even now but when my view changed in college, I was blessed with an amazing support system of women who are my village. I was able to share my stories of hurt, sadness, loneliness, success, joy, and love. I could be myself.

The other night, I saw Madame Butterfly with one of my dearest girlfriends. As I watched the amazing performances, I realized that this dated opera still had implications for women today. Like Butterfly, we have sat by the window of life, waiting for years for the ship to come in. It is on that ship that we will find the love and happiness that we desire. Sadly, many of us die on swords created by our jaded illusions of life. We might not be in charge of all that happens in life but we do have the ability to accept or reject anything that happens to us. In waiting for our ship to come in, as many women before us have done, we give up our power and give it to others. When I discovered I was a woman was when I chose to claim and own my power. I became a woman when I changed the way I saw myself, saw other women as strong and powerful, and when I saw that I have a special place in this world. I became a woman when I surrounded myself with other powerful women without feeling intimidated or insecure. I became a woman when I decided that I had to take each issue that was on the shelf, address it with love and make healing and wholeness the goal for me, for my ancestors and the women to come in the future. I became a woman when I found my voice and began to tell my truth to others.

*"Women have to work much harder to make it in this world. It really pisses me off that women don't get the same opportunities as men do, or money for that matter. Because let's face it, money gives men the power to run the show. It gives men the power to define our values and to define what's sexy and what's feminine and that's bullshit. At the end of the day, it's not about equal rights, it's about how we think. We have to reshape our own perception of how we view ourselves." — Beyoncé*

## **Notes**

1. Quotation from Michelle Obama

2. Quotation from Beyonce Knowles

## You Can't Make This Shit Up!
## by
## Wendy Winegardner

    As I reflect on my life and try to pinpoint when I became a woman, I realized that a series of events has lead me to become who I am. I had to become the woman that my mother is not. I had to prove to myself that I am strong enough to break her hold on me. You know, it's a constant struggle in my life that my actions are NOT like the abuse that was endured by me and my siblings. Writing this essay, about becoming a woman, is most certainly cathartic for me and perhaps it will be for someone else. I want to take you on a cleansing journey about how these memories of different events allowed me to develop different parts of my being. Going through these tragedies allowed me to become the woman that I am today.
    While I was reflecting, I think back to when my mother had a twisted way of disciplining my sister and I. My ability to question people, situations, and circumstances came from my mother pinning us to the bed. Yes, pinned with old school diaper pins. Apparently, my sister and I had circus time. We were all over the room in the bedroom that we shared. In an attempt to keep us in our own beds, my mother pinned our underwear to the sheets. We were too young to think about wiggling out of them and be free.
 I remember, however, thinking why would my mom do this to us? This began my questioning things and ideas of others through the lens of is there a better way. Of course, with my mother there was not but it has helped me to delve deeper into what a situation may bring. I do not make hasty decisions. I am very conscientious and deliberate when making choices for me and my family.

Learning to laugh through the pain was my superpower. Being paddled evoked my sense of humor. For example, drawing mustaches on the faces of people in the parish directory was frowned upon by my parents, as it should be. I was literally bored at home and thought that drawing would make the time go by faster. As I looked down at my masterpiece, my mother looked down at the directory and was infuriated. What was amazing to me was that I was being forced to bend over the couch and take the strikes to our bare bottoms. It always seemed ironic to me that we (my sisters and I) were literally beaten for being creative. Here is my questioning piece of my personality - Was it really necessary to beat a kid for drawing mustaches? Couldn't there have been worse things my sisters and I should have gotten beaten for- not drawing in a church directory that would be thrown out the next year? Geez, I had to laugh through that and much more that was coming in my life.

Resiliency came when I endured the struggle of being the daughter of the most hated parents in my grade school and parish, for that matter. Other parishioners knew how evil my parents were. My parents thought they were among the highly respected. In reality, they were among the most detested. I remembered the whispers of the other women and men as my parents walked about. As we attended the parish school, where everyone knew our parents did not take great care of us, I remember sobbing as I tried to find matching hand-me-down socks. This was very detrimental because children were cruel and not having the same type of socks on would have meant belittlement and ridicule. I remember dreaming of Nike or Adidas tennis shoes so I could "be like" the other girls. Trying to fit in with the other girls, I desperately wanted to cut my long hair. My mother refused because mother wanted her 3 girls to look exactly like her. Once I came to the realization that is not your physical appearance that makes a person who they are, it's what's in a person's heart, I began to get my strength back from being the poor little child to a child who has promise.

Through consequence and circumstance, I gained my ability to smile through the pain. I was often backhand slapped for speaking up for myself. You see, I spent hours upon hours at the kitchen table listening to the diatribe of a woman who delighted in making herself feel superior to her children. If I spoke or questioned her, I was smacked and then told to smile. The sting of the hit hurt so bad that I would literally smile through my tears. This has helped me disguise my true feelings and emotions so that I don't let people see me sweat or flinch when I am being crucified. I don't allow others to get me because I smile through the pain.

My sense of knowing right from wrong came at Christmas. Picking out the tree always was tense. My mother never went to pick a tree out, yet expected perfection in the form of a Norman Rockwell tree. Pushing, shoving and screaming were the results of picking the wrong tree. Decorating the tree had to match her vision, or the tree was done over and over and over. My mother sat and directed. What a treat it was picking up the pine needles from the floor and receiving **one** of her prized Velamints, a small square shaped mint, as a reward. We didn't even receive nice presents and what should be heightened anticipation of Christmas always was horrifying.

I learned how to be a servant to others. I was awakened at the crack of dawn to begin cleaning house while my mother went back to bed. I dug weeds out of sidewalk cracks with a screwdriver which bloodied my knuckles. I picked dead leaves one by one out of the ivy bed. I washed and dried household plant leaves. I answered my mother's whistle or bell when she needed something, as she lay in her bed. I was one of 3 dishwashers (my two sisters and I). Oh how she delighted in saying that she had three dishwashers to her so called friends who pitied us. I understand the nature of being taught responsibility, as I have done that for my own children, but doing these chores would have been easier had my mother held a job or made dinner or made our lunches or did laundry or clean or did something to contribute to the common good of the family. She did not. She lay in her bed or on an air mattress in the pool ALL day long waiting to be waited upon.

    I learned how to be strong. I literally **begged** for help after having an unexpected C-section with my daughter. They would not alter (by one week) their two month Florida vacation plans as they "already paid" for their accommodations. Keep in mind, they were and are financially stable. This was justified this of course by gifting us a Thanksgiving meal. I realized at that point that my daughter needed me regardless of my physical limitations and I had to be strong for her.

    I am not a spoiled brat complaining about my childhood, as I realize that every family has their challenges. This is a glimpse into what it is like growing up with a narcissistic mother, and how I chose to grow as a woman from my experiences. I learned everything by doing the opposite of her example. She is still alive and living her dream in the desert without contact from me or my sisters. That speaks volumes of her inability to love and of my ability to rise as a stronger woman.

I AM WOMAN: Defining Womanhood and Identity

*BRAVERY*

## "Take It Like a Woman-Take Twelve"

### by

### Dr. Monique Maxey

**Trigger Warning**

As I began contemplating the idea of defining womanhood for myself, the first thought was a statement uttered to me when I was 12 years old. In fact, the contemplation took me beyond the statement, to a series of events that happened during the entire year. When I was 12, my Pentecostal mother began to emphasize that 12 was the age Jesus preached his first sermon. In other words, for her, age 12 symbolized the beginning of maturation. She consistently laid out expectations to be held now that I was 12. She was preparing me to transition from girlhood to womanhood, including the physical and mental challenges that lie ahead. For example, 12 was the age she felt I could learn the truth about my daddy: he was not "working" out of town, but incarcerated. These were truths that somehow, I was supposed to be able to tolerate because I was at the age you begin to put down childish things. Achieving age 12 set the stage for a great deal to come.

One of the salient occurrences during the year was when she told me this was the last year she would buy me a baby doll for Christmas. This last baby doll was surely a special one. It was a My Child, which was a popular doll which came out in the 80s. They were supposedly more diverse and designed to look like you. The "problem" I had as a light skinned black girl with hair with red hair is that the red-headed white baby looked more like me than the toffee colored black baby with the coal black hair. For the first time (and last time) my mother bought me a white baby doll. After all, she had nothing against them. She just wanted to make sure her daughters developed a love for their own varied hues and saw themselves represented in their toys before becoming idolized with a blond-haired, blue-eyed Barbie. She bought the My Child and I was both sad and happy, knowing this would be my last baby doll. I did not know if I wanted to grow up.

Yet my body was betraying me, despite my youthful face. Somehow during the year, I transitioned to wearing a 32D cup. A grown woman's bra size. I also recall starting my period during the year. I remembered because I was the youngest of my friends and the youngest to receive my period. When I told my best friend at the time I was absent from school because I started my period, she laughed and called me a baby. After all, she had been having hers for almost 2 years now. Well damn it, I still was a baby!

Around this time, I also remembered young Mila Jovovich was becoming very popular as a supermodel. She looked quite mature for her age. One of my friends compared me to her since we were both 12, asking why I did not look like this? I retorted back that she was 14, and she still did not look like her. Me:1 Her: 0. Twelve meant tumultuous times for me. I was growing older. My body looked grown. But inside, I was still a kid who had no idea what being a woman meant.

I do not know if it was turning 12. I do not know if it was that summer. All I know is that it was a watershed point in my life. I was selected to be among a group of children in the neighborhood summer camp. I do not recall the name of the group. I remember we were chosen as the best behaved and brightest stars of the camp to travel around the city and become exposed to a variety of cultural activities. Spruce up and expose the ghetto kids was the mission du jour of the day. I happened to be the youngest of the group, but probably one of the smartest. The others were in high school; however, I was going to the eighth grade. I was mature and well behaved, so my dance teacher advocated for me to have this chance. I was granted the opportunity, and performed quite well with the 'big kids.'

The culmination of the program was a weekend stay at one of the fanciest hotels in the city. One of the first things you want to do as a child is swim in the hotel swimming pool. We were excited to do so! Only after I went swimming, I was not excited anymore. One of the older boys started to grope me. Boys had grabbed my nonexistent butt before, and tried to touch my ample-for-my-age breasts. They do this, you chase and slap them. It was the dialectical dance between the sexes. However, this was different. This was aggressive. He physically grabbed me between my legs. Hard. I was so confused, and I did not like it. I felt violated. Yet the older girls were acting like I was supposed to like it. So, do I coyly smile or kick him in the nuts? Because I really wanted the latter to occur. But in this confusing time of girl-becoming-woman, what do I do?

As the evening progressed, I was getting ready for bed with my three other older roommates. The oldest was anointed Chaperone by Proxy. Yet she was not concerned much about violating the rules. See at 12, you are still concerned with following rules. She was 16-not so much. There was a 14-year-old girl in our room who wanted to have sex with The Groper's older brother, and called for him to sneak into our room. Here was the catch-The Groper wanted to come to the room for me. Since she wanted the older brother, she traded me off like I was an item at the local flea market. I begged her to at least let me put on clothes, because I only had on a nightshirt and panties. Alas, it was too late. She gave Big Brother the go ahead, and they were down by the door quicker than she could hang up. I jumped in my bed and pulled the cover under me, along with the girl I shared the bed.

We were creating an impenetrable defense. "He's not going to be able to infiltrate the covers, or he'll get bored from trying," I thought/prayed to myself. He burst in and went straight for our bed. We had on our game plan. However, this was no regular 14-year-old boy. He played varsity football. He was bigger and stronger than me. Eventually, I was no match for him. He was also wearing down my one ally.

The 14-year-old girl was busy in the bathroom. Chaperone by Proxy called for The Groper, who sauntered over and flirted with her for a nanosecond. She, however, was not who he wanted. She was willing to give it up to him, but he did not want it easy. He wanted it rough and by force. So, he circled back around toward me. I was afraid if I resisted any more, he would hurt me. He wrestled the cover with determination and fought off the two of us. There was no more barrier between he and I. Then Chaperone by Proxy uttered those words:

"Take it like a woman!"

I will never forget those words. I had a multitude of questions on the absurdity of her statement. How does a woman take it? Am I not a woman? Is this what makes me a woman? Does this mean I will walk out of here a woman? Well I was not ready to become a woman that day.

That year, perhaps even more specifically that moment, marked the beginning of my transition to womanhood. Truthfully, it would not be years later until I experienced other phenomena supposedly associated with being a woman. Definitively, I do not recall the epiphany when I realized I was a woman. However, I can tell you I realized what being a woman meant for me. It did not include looking a certain way, or engaging in adult activities.

Being raped in a room full of my peers was not what made me a woman. I hastily went to sleep, wishing this was a horrific nightmare which would dissolve in the morning. When the morning came and I discovered my blood-stained panties, I did not feel automatically inducted into the Secret Society of Women. After this painful violation occurred, I still had to face The Groper Now Turned Rapist. I had to face the other children on the bus, including my very own suitemates who, knowingly or otherwise, were complicit in a sexual assault. I had to face the authentically adult chaperones, who may or may not have known what was going on.

I had a decision to make. Becoming a woman was a reaching a conclusion partially decided by me, partially decided for me. I decided to confront and negotiate a situation no child of 12 should ever have to face. Becoming a woman was when I discovered I would have to tell that the disgustingly vile deed happened.

I made the decision to tell, because I was paranoid everyone knew. I was more concerned about my dance teacher knowing above everyone else. Well if she was going to know, I wanted to make sure she knew I did not do it willingly. I wanted her to know it was forced and how hard I tried to prevent it from happening. If I was not able to control what happened, I wanted to control the narrative with the truth. I had to recount the story in front of every parent who had a child who attended the field trip, as well as the camp administrators. I began to realize a woman confronts that which was intended to break her, rising from the circumstance a wiser person.

Chaperone-In-Proxy's mother questioned my authenticity. She had a stake in this-her daughter was given a semi-supervisory role. In my narrative, her daughter turned from responsible teenager to criminal accomplice. She tried to rewrite my narrative, turning fact into fiction. She sided with The Groper's mother, stating I did not appear traumatized enough. I knew more than anything, I wanted to return to The Land Where Children Played. During breaks from my interrogation (a more accurate description), I went outside and played around with one of the administrators' son. He was a kind face. He was my age, and he reminded me of a return to love. You could tell he was still a child, and you could feel his kindness, warmth, and empathy. Of course, I'd rather play with him, than to sit in a room full of adults attempting to slut shame me. My only hero was my mother, and she had to tend to the grown-up talk of defending me. However, my attempt at normalcy, at achieving homeostasis, at receiving any kindness was confronted with the suspicion I may be an elaborate fabricator.

The second hardest decision was not to accept anyone else's interpolation of events of my life as true, simply because it made them feel better. I learned, or at least solidified The Art of the Pushback. This woman was not only trying to lie and paint me in a promiscuous light to alleviate her situation; she was simultaneously trying to make herself and her child look better at my expense. I could see this and politely, respectfully, but firmly rejected these alternative facts. My mother sensed what was going on and navigated the terrain more adeptly, while modeling the art form for me.

I am not suggesting everyone should experience hardship to become a woman. This road is unfortunately one that appeared along my journey. However, in life I realize no matter where you come from, you will receive lemons in life. And through the process of making garden variety lemonade or an elegant lemon soufflé, you become a woman. You learn what you will stand up for, where your boundaries are, what you will and you will not take. And you will constantly refine it and discern who you are, and what you will believe. There will be more knowledge attained and more lessons learned.

For years, I have refined and perfected this task. I have not held roles which many assume fold into the identity of being a woman, as women of the world are indeed caretakers and nurturers. I have never been a wife, though I have performed wifely duties I suppose. I have never been a mother, though I have helped raise children on this earth. Women are identified in relation to others, often spouses and children, as if their identities are malleable or indistinguishable from their charges. They become subsumed under these roles, until it becomes a difficult task to tease them apart.

The bridge from girlhood to womanhood is often built on the backs of the early sexualization, domestication, and even the deflowering of young girls. Much of the definition of womanhood also becomes absorbed in this process. However, the definition of womanhood lies independent of our spouses or children. Especially given many women achieve the task of becoming woman without engaging in any of these roles. As hard as it may be for society to conceive, the role of a woman is an independent one. Even if the woman decides to include those roles into her identity, it is her choice to make, and hers alone. "Mrs. Jones" or "Tasha's mama" has a name. She has an identity. A story. A voice. A journey.

Womanhood is the journey one takes in discovering who you are. Of what sturdy stuff you are made. Although most believe it is attained when you are the age of a chronological adult, womanhood continues throughout life. Instead of linear, it is three dimensional and it is quite formidable. It is learning to harness the innate power which resides in you.

Recalibrating the world's lightning into your own personal electric source. Whether the journey has been smooth, or it has been rough filled with detours, it remains the same for us all. Womanhood revolves in the choices, especially those unique to gender, one must make for herself to successfully navigate the vicissitudes of this temporary thing called life. The older I become, the more enriching the journey becomes. As the old adage goes, the best is yet to come.

## **Notes**

The trigger warning was given due to the nature and content of this piece. If you need help, please go to your nearest emergency room or contact a counselor, therapist, or someone in the mental health field. You are too precious to lose.

**National Suicide Hotline**
**1-800-273-8255**

## OVERCOMING

# The Pearls of My DNA
## by
## Dawn Warren

The four women who inspired me to be the proud and independent woman I am today are my great-grandmother (Emma Lou Isles-Yates), my grandmother (Martha Yates), my great aunt (Edith Dixon) and my mother (Sandra Warren). My inspiration for who I am as a woman is embroidered throughout my family DNA through their beauty, wisdom, distinction and love.

I am deeply connected to the roots of who I am. The generations of DNA that make up the essence of 'this' woman also inspire the essence of my womanhood. Each of these four women are characterized as pearls of Beauty, Wisdom, Distinction and Love and I've uniquely inherited each one of their traits.

The first pearl of beauty and key to my heart was my great-grandmother, Emma Lou Iles-Yates. A lot of my childhood was spent with my great-grandmother who taught me to put Christ first, be caring and nurturing and to enjoy each moment of my life. Emma Lou Isles-Yates represented everything that was good in the world. Her kind, humble and gentle spirit made everyone in her presence feel welcome and at home. Her smile and sweet voice was enough to brighten up anyone's day. My great-grandfather adored her! She spent a lot of time sharing her family history with me and teaching me about who I am. As a woman, I embrace the gentleness and beauty of her spirit that dwells within me. It's defined by my core values, my soul, and who I am as a woman. Her legacy continues as I pick up the torch to discover more about myself through my family's history. As a woman, I have such an appreciation for my heritage and my great-grandmother's humble spirit that resides within me. She taught me that the true essence of beauty lies within one's soul and to never forget that God is Love. I am thankful to my great-grandmother for being in my life.

The second pearl of wisdom in my life and my beacon of strength derived from my maternal grandmother, Martha Yates, who I affectionately called, "Granny". My grandmother taught me a lot about life's lessons beginning with how to put Christ first and how to work with my hands. As a small child, she taught me to revere the Bible and I quickly learned that it was inappropriate to dance to church music the way you do to secular music. To this day, I clap my hands and pat my feet to the beat. My grandparents owned a farm so I learned a lot from watching my grandmother use her hands to sow and till her vegetable garden and she taught me how to cook. My grandmother made sure I understood that having livestock is where the concept of grocery store food originated and that healthy food came from the earth. In addition to life on the farm, my grandmother was a seamstress and a very hard worker. She instilled a hard work ethic in me to always give 100% effort to my studies and occupation. I'm from a small town community and Granny encouraged me to learn more about black history because it wasn't taught at my school. It became my mission to read and learn more so that I could later incorporate black history into my future lesson plans. My grandmother encouraged me to research our family history so that I could learn more about my roots and the strength that my loved ones had to endure during slavery. The information gathered from this extensive research gave me a deep appreciation of all my many blessings. It was then that I realized that my goals and dreams were bigger than myself. Everyone that came before me (whether they were kin or not) did not have the same opportunities as me but struggled so that I could attain them. Knowledge is power! I was determined to set high goals and accomplish them. Knowing my history (black history and heritage) and the skills my grandmother taught me and inspired me, to make healthy choices for my life and to follow my dreams. I pursued an education major in a foreign language at college and studied in a foreign country. In 1998, I became the First African-American ESOL Teacher in the state of Missouri. My school district was the first to bring it to my attention. This was the same year that my grandmother passed away but I know she would've been proud of me. As a woman, I'm filled with the pride of my family's legacy and I don't take anything for granted. I have a great appreciation for nature and respect that only good things come from the earth. I appreciate the small things in life and I give 100% in everything I do. It is my mission to teach my international students to be proud of their heritage and culture. I am thankful to my grandmother for giving me wisdom.

The third pearl of distinction in my life is my great-aunt, Edith Dixon, affectionately known as Aunt Edith. Since my paternal grandmother passed away before I was born, I spent a lot of summers during my childhood with her younger sister. Aunt Edith was very involved in the Baptist Church as a Choir Director and usher. We spent a lot of time praising God in worship and she made it her mission to teach me the Lord's Prayer and my own personal scripture, Psalm

23[1], to recite before every meal.  She was very elegant and spent a lot time showing me how to become a young lady.  It was her passion trying to teach me how to mix and match clothing, shoes and accessories.  I truly admired her style but struggle with the look of sophistication and finesse today.  It's time-consuming but all jokes aside, I know how to be sophisticated.  There were times when I felt ugly and was disgusted with the bumps on my legs.  I was often teased but my Aunt Edith taught me how to speak up for myself and always made me feel beautiful inside and out.  Although she enjoyed spoiling me, she taught me how to be giving and accepting of others.  Whenever I smell the sweet fragrance of Estee Lauder, I automatically think of Aunt Edith.  She was very sophisticated and knew how to capture one's attention.  As a polished woman, I strive to work on this area of my life more and more each day.  The scent and sophistication of a woman is the key to loving oneself and for me, attracting the love I desire my way.  I am thankful to my great-aunt for being a wonderful role model and teaching me that it's wonderful to "stand out" and be uniquely made as a woman.

Last but certainly not least in my life is the special pearl of Love, known as my mother, Sandra Warren.  As a child, my mother taught me the importance of putting God first, stepping outside my comfort zone, setting and reaching my goals, and to strive for ambition in my life.  As a child, my mom taught me how to get down on my knees and pray to God each night before I go to bed.  She was a Sunday school teacher and she would teach me about the different Bible stories so that I would have a spiritual foundation.  As a spiritual woman, I've been baptized twice (as a Methodist and Baptist) and I'm certified in Evangelism.  I know who I am and whose I am.  My mother felt it was important for me to step outside my comfort zone and get involved in activities. As a shy child, I was not interested in softball or Girl Scouts, etc. My sister was taking tap dancing lessons and rehearsing for the Miss Teen Missouri Pageant. My mother insisted that I choose some activities but I wasn't stepping outside my comfort zone so she made the selections for me; softball and Girl Scouts were assigned to me. She would wait patiently for me after softball practice while one of the baseball players taught me how to swing a bat. Although I was just out in right field passing time, I was actually a pretty good hitter to my own amazement. I remember hitting a homerun and my whole family cheering me around each base. It was a shock to my central nervous system to hear everyone say, "Run, Dawn, Run!" As Steve Urkel would say, "Did I do that?". I never would've known what I was capable of if I hadn't stepped outside my comfort zone. As a Girl Scout in 1977, I remember shaking hands with President Carter. In 1991, I would get the chance to meet and shake hands with Governor Bill Clinton. Little did I know that Governor Clinton would become the 42nd President of the United States of America. I'm thankful that my mother encouraged me to step outside my comfort zone. In high school, I would try out for cheerleading, dance squad, speech and drama and with lots of practice would excel at all three activities. My mother would attend basketball games just to see me dance and cheer, and she never missed a play or musical. She became my biggest supporter and taught me how to be a champion supporter of others. In high school, I was still an introvert but I was learning to "stand out" and try new things as the only black girl in some of these activities. It taught me to have a "thick skin". I had to step out of my comfort zone from Kindergarten through high school because I didn't have a choice. I was from a small town and I was one of 36 students in my class. Over the years, I had to tolerate ignorance but I also learned how to be accepting of others. After all, my family wasn't planning on moving from our small town. As a mature woman, I've learned to appreciate the solitude and close-knit bond of my hometown community. When life gets stressful, it's become my getaway. My mother always told me that I would need to work twice as hard as my classmates in school. Her desire was to be an English Teacher. As a child, she was the first person to teach me how to read and write. All of my Cabbage Patch dolls came from different countries so I spent a lot of time teaching them to read and write, as well. As a young woman, I worked hard to make the honor roll in high school and the Dean's List in college. My ambition led me to earn a foreign language scholarship to study abroad. Although my mother wasn't fond of me leaving the country, she encouraged me to work hard and adhere to the rules abroad so that I could make it back home. As of today, I teach English as a Second Language to students representing 20 different countries in grades Kindergarten through 5th grade. I've taught high school Spanish I, II, III & IV and currently teaching a parent and child Spanish class. My goal is to teach a citizenship class this summer to migrant workers from Mexico. As God continues to move mountains in my life, I strive to keep him first. I am thankful to my mother for the love she has bestowed upon me. She moved beyond her comfort zone to allow me the opportunities I have today.

I am a proud, independent and strong black woman full of beauty, wisdom, distinction and love thanks to my great-grandmother, grandmother, great aunt, and most of all, my mother. Each of these women are a treasured pearl and define the woman I am today.

## **Notes**

1. Scriptures King James Version
   Psalm 23 Zondervan Publishing, 2017

## MIRACLES

## Miracles and Blessings
## *D*amn, *I*'m *V*ictorious *A*lways (D.I.V. A.)
## By
## Kimberley Jones, MA

*Trust in the LORD with all thine heart: and lean not unto thine own understanding. In all thy ways acknowledge him, and he shall direct thy paths.*
*Proverbs 3:5-6*[1]

When I was asked to write an essay about an inspirational life event, I knew I had to give a testimony.

I have been married twice and divorced twice! I was married to my *first* husband for 15 years and my *second* husband for 15 months. My first husband was one year older than me whereas my second husband was 19 years older than me. We would call my first husband "H" and my second husband "J".

While I was married to H, we went through fertility treatments for TWO YEARS to have a baby. I was informed by the "experts" that the reason we were unable to have a baby was because I was not able to ovulate. However, H's reproductive system was just fine. This was very devastating due to my wanting a child. I thought becoming a woman was not just worth or accomplishments, but giving life.

After my divorce from H, I met my second husband, J. J only had *one* child with his first wife and that child was in his 30's. Due to the experts, I knew I could have any children. Being my second husband's forth wife, he believed that he could not have any children either. At that time of my life, we were both over the road truck drivers. While driving, I became nausea and thought it was motion sickness. I did not know what was going on with me.

Unbeknownst to me, I became pregnant with my FIRST and ONLY child. When I found out that I was pregnant, I was in my fourth month! I was considered a high-risk pregnancy due to being an older mother at age 40 but GOD brought both us through without any problems. **On May 22, 2008, I gave birth by cesarean section to my beautiful baby girl that I named *after* me, Kimberley.**

If I would have stayed with H even after him choosing to make a different decision about our relationship, I would not have had my daughter-especially since I had to have a total hysterectomy due to medical problems. In addition, H still does NOT have any children but the "experts" said that he was fine.

What I learned was to TRUST IN THE LORD! My faith in God made me a woman. This is when I became whole. I was a woman before, but I realized that I was a **DIVA- Damn, I'm Victorious Always**, I was told by "experts" that I would never be able to conceive but GOD SAID THAT I WOULD and I DID! Many times we block our own blessings by not having FAITH. Trust and believe in HIM and HE will direct your path. AMEN

## *REBIRTH*

## *A Higher Vision*
## *by*
## *Queen Leia Lewis*

When I was twenty-six years old, I had an ego-shattering spiritual breakthrough of self-realization. For several years, I had been living a respectable and successful life as a single young professional. In fact, since my childhood, I had followed the honorable and praise worthy steps of social advancement. Upon graduating from a top ranking academic high school, I earned a full ride scholarship to college, then progressed to graduate school and a rising career in the field of arts. Furthermore, I had purchased my first home at the age of twenty-one. Yet, even with these achievements, over time, I became aware of a constantly nagging sense of unease and restlessness.

To the best of my understanding then, I felt that something was missing from my life; and I constantly wondered what it was. I confessed my concerns to God and prayed for guidance. Then one unforeseen night, my prayers were answered. In the flash of a moment, the very course of my life changed.

Starting off with a typical Friday of partying with my friends, we had a full evening of club hopping, dancing, and pleasure seeking, I returned home late after midnight. I fumbled my way through the silent rooms of my house and landed in bed. And as I lay there, I was confronted with a looming thought:

**WHAT ARE YOU DOING WITH YOUR LIFE?**

I was astounded by the question and turned the idea over in my mind. I thought to myself, *"God. What am I doing with my life?"*

In my early twenties, I was a complex personality. By outward appearance, I was a successful young lady who was easygoing, culturally proud, professionally in charge, creatively passionate, and deeply spiritual. Yet, I also harbored contradictions to my external image. For example, I struggled with being self-confident and I judged myself harshly against impossible standards of perfection. I, also, had made a series of poor choices in relationships. My vices and self-sabotaging behaviors were flawed attempts to deal with my frustration, heartbreak, and discontent. At my core, I was unsettled, ungrounded, and unfulfilled.

Inebriated and smelling of bar smoke, I reached for a book on my nightstand. I felt compelled to search my well-worn copy of <u>Tapping the Power Within</u> by Iyanla Vanzant[1]. After flipping through the pages, I mustered the focus and intention to finally do a healing ritual I had been resistant to complete called *Looking in the Mirror of Self*.

Reading the book aloud, I followed the process. So, I stripped off my clothes and stood naked in front of the floor length mirror hanging on my closet door. I scanned my body from head to toe, sizing myself up. Then, I moved in closely and examined my face. At first, looking at my reflection seemed routine and forced. Yet, the more deeply that I looked in my eyes, the greater I yearned to see.

I prayed to God to show me myself. I asked and pleaded to see my TRUE SELF. I searched my eyes with a fiery intensity and shouted, *"I see the truth of who I am! I see the truth of who I am. I see the truth of who I am!"* As I repeated the mantra with my gaze fixed on the mirror, the energy flashed and shifted.

In a transcendent moment of clarity, I saw

beyond my image and connected with my soul. I saw that I was a sad girl who was in pain. Hot, bitter tears streamed down my face. Then I wondered why I hadn't seen myself this way before. Suddenly, a new awareness flashed in my consciousness:

**YOU ARE A COWARD.**

I was caught off guard by the words. The message sobered me instantly. I searched my memory for the definition of a coward. A person who is easily frightened, spineless, dishonest, paralyzed by fear, and pathetic is a coward.

I quickly processed and rejected the idea.
*"WHAT? A COWARD...NOT ME!"*
The very word – coward - offended my sensibility. My mind raced to defend my identity. I have earned a Master's Degree. I am the Assistant Director of a prestigious organization. I am a home owner. Blah, Blah, Blah. My mind ticked off reason after reason why I was far too good to be a coward.

And with the stealth quickness of an eagle, Divine Spirit snatched my ego and convicted me. In my Spirit, I clearly heard plainly:

**YES, YOU ARE A COWARD.**

**YOU DREAM OF TRAVELING THE WORLD...**

**YOU SAY WANT TO CREATE ART AND TO BE A FREE SPIRIT...**

**HOWEVER, YOU DO NOTHING ABOUT IT...**

**YOU HAVE MADE NO SERIOUS EFFORT TO MAKE YOUR DREAMS REAL...**

**YOU ARE A COWARD.**

When you receive a spiritual revelation, the spirit is potent and pure. When the Most High blesses you with crystal clear understanding, your mind can be renewed in an instant. I had to admit that the messages were correct. Yes, I was a coward. Yes, I was sad. Yes, I was hurting. And, yes, I was too scared to live my life fully and freely. I collapsed to the floor confronted by the powerful weight of these insights into my character.

Naked and stripped of illusions, I cried my heart out and lay there sobbing. Years of pent up emotions poured out. With each tear, I mourned the loss of my identity. I was a snotty, tear streaked, hot mess.

I looked over my twenty-six years of life and wondered, *"Who am I, really?"* For so long, I had defined myself and my value by my productive work ethic, my career accomplishments, and my ability to excel under pressure. However, I knew that returning to my former life of being a proper, predictable young professional with reckless tendencies was not a viable option. My future was unknown. Yet, I knew one thing for certain. That is, I was ready to get serious about my desire to travel the world.

I picked myself up from the floor and noticed that I felt lighter and clearer. I looked in the mirror, deep into my eyes, and there I was - Refreshed, free of self judgement, and hopeful about my life. As I stood before the mirror gazing at my reflection, a smile spread across my face and laughter bubbled from my core. A fresh awareness dawned on me:

**GOD IS WITH ME. SO LONG AS I HAVE BREATH, I AM BLESSED WITH THE OPPORTUNITY TO MAKE NEW AND DIFFERENT CHOICES. MY DREAMS ARE POSSIBLE. I CAN HAVE WHAT I DESIRE.**

Fast forward several months following my spiritual breakthrough, I had quit my job and embarked on an inspired journey that led me to Jamaica, Cuba, and back to my hometown in Louisiana. At the time, I could never have guessed the adventures I would experience, the phenomenal people who I would connect with, and how I was destined to make a special mark on the world through my unique path as a cultural worker, community builder, teacher, artist, entrepreneur, healer, and mother.

Today, more than two decades later, I now am a woman in my forties. Through many challenging and richly rewarding life experiences, I am still growing and expanding. I have learned that when a woman confronts and heals her fears, pain, and limiting beliefs, she will continuously discover new dimensions of her spiritual gifts, her passions, and her divine purpose. Indeed, I bear witness that one of the most important prayers is this:

**GOD, SHOW ME TRUTH OF WHO I AM.**

On the night that I had the courage to "look in the mirror of self," my identity radically shifted from being an insecure, people-pleasing girl. Instead, I accessed my TRUE SELF - and I stepped into my power to be authentic and create a joyful life. This is when I realized that I had become a woman.

# **Notes**

1. Iyanla Vanzant. *Tapping the power within: A path to self-empowerment for women.* Hay House, 1992.

ABOUT THE AUTHORS
**FEATURED AUTHORS ARE BOLDED**

# Dr. Camesha Hill-Carter, Editor-in-Chief

Dr. Camesha Hill-Carter is a professional speaker, motivational author, world changer, successful entrepreneur and life coach, who help individuals and organizations achieve their potential by inspiring the individual to accentuate, build and calibrate professional, private and personal relationships. An observer of human nature, Camesha noticed that there is a method in developing one's potential. Being resourceful and optimistic, Camesha went on her quest to solving the question "How can I help people understand the limitless opportunities that awaits them?" As she delivered topics and expressed possibilities, epiphany struck, and "Live Your Destiny Now™" was born.

From that day forward, the acknowledgement mantra became a guiding principle on how to harness the dream and power on the inside of a person and unleash the full magnitude of its essence into the world. Constantly relating to people, from all walks of life, Camesha emits confidence to those who need it, gives care to those who want it and the truth to those who desire it. Her charismatic style, mother wit and courageous stance draw you into the path you are to be on, moves you through your potential and into your destiny. Passionately, Dr. Hill-Carter walks with you through fear and helps you to conquer your obstacles that stand on the path of your journey.

Dr. Hill-Carter's training is vast and varied. Growing up in a drug infested neighborhood in Shreveport, LA, Camesha rose through the ranks of education, while teachers and faculty called her inept, ignorant and impossible to deal with. She conquered those criticisms and received her Doctorate of Education (Ed.D) in Educational Administration in 2010; being first in both family lines to work toward such an accomplishment.

Starting in customer service as a teenager, Camesha worked in the corporate arena through college. Camesha became an educator and trainer through the tutelage of Louisiana State University-Shreveport. Seeing the need for more comprehensive leadership, Dr. Hill-Carter received her Master's in Reading and English as a Second Language from Centenary College of Louisiana and a certificate in Administration from Lindenwood University.

Dr. Camesha Hill-Carter joined Delta Sigma Theta Sorority in the Spring of 1992 on the campus of Louisiana State University- Shreveport. As a faithful member of her collegiate chapter, Pi Pi, Camesha served as chapter historian, recording secretary, corresponding secretary, member of the Minerva Circle and chaplain. Through her travels she has been a member of Shreveport Alumnae, Grambling Alumnae, East Saint Louis Alumnae and her home St. Louis Metropolitan Alumnae. Her leadership includes National Chaplains' Council, Alternate Delegate for 1993 Regional Conference, Regional Chaplains' Council, DID trainer, Sisterhood Committee Coordinator and Co-chaplain for St. Louis Metropolitan Alumnae. Dr. Hill-Carter served on several committees and worked with many others which include Social Action, Arts and Letters, Education, Scholarship, Metro Melodies and Rites of Passage. She served on the Luncheon Logistic and Registration Committees for the 2011 Regional Conference. Dr. Carter's crowning achievement in Delta thus far was the keynote speaker for the 2012-2013 Scholarship Social. Dr. Carter is looking forward to continue to serve her chapter and the sorority diligence, dignity and decorum.

As an award winning author, Dr. Hill-Carter has written for Women of Excellence Magazine, Teaching K-8 and Learning Magazine. She also penned several books I Was Lied To: Debunking The Happily Ever After Myth. Proverbs 31 Woman, Live Your Destiny Now™: Understanding Who You Are and Fire Up™ 30 Strategies On Firing Up Your Potential And Living Your Destiny Now. She is also a contributor to the book Black Male Teachers: Diversifying the United States Teacher Workforce. Currently Camesha is completing her 4th book I DARE YOU: 30 Days to Fire Up Your Potential and Live Your Destiny Now!

Currently, Dr. Carter works with homeless women to coach them in life skills as well as building their ego after their tragic experiences. She also works with students who are considered to be "lost" on anger management and behavior management.

Dr. Carter emerges as one of the country's leading expert on Empowerment for individuals, small and medium businesses. After hours of observing human behaviors, Camesha found a common theme; all human behavior is motivated. Using that thought, Dr. Hill-Carter developed a program that will help individuals and organizations find the disconnect and move forward on their goal, dream or destiny. You may contact Dr. Carter at camesha@cameshacarter.com or www.cameshacarter.com.

## Dr. Froswa Booker-Drew

Froswa' Booker-Drew, PhD has an extensive background in nonprofit management, partnership development, training and education. She is currently  the Director of Community Affairs/Strategic Alliances for the State Fair of Texas. Formerly the National Community Engagement Director for World Vision, she served as a catalyst, partnership broker, and builder of the capacity of local partners in multiple locations across the US to improve and sustain the well-being of children and their families. She is the recipient of several honors including 2014 Alpha Kappa Alpha Global Heart Award, 2012 Outstanding African American Alumni Award from the University of Texas at Arlington, 2009 Woman of the Year Award by Zeta Phi Beta Sorority, Inc. and Diversity Ambassador for the American Red Cross. Froswa' graduated with a PhD from Antioch University in Leadership and Change with a focus on social capital and relational leadership. She is the author of two workbooks for women, Ready for a Revolution: 30 Days to Jolt Your Life and Rules of Engagement: Making Connections Last. She was a Post-Doctoral Fellow at Antioch University and is an adjunct professor at Lancaster Bible College/Capital Seminary and the University of North Texas-Dallas. She is a writer for several publications around the world.

## *Andrea Stumon Claiborne, MA*

Andrea Stumon Claiborne was born 1973 in Shreveport, Louisiana. She is a God-fearing wife, mother of three children, daughter, and sister. She is a 1991 graduate of Fair Park High School in Shreveport, Louisiana. She briefly served in the United States Air Force. Andrea has over twenty years' experience in customer service which includes employment in the telecommunications industry. Her most challenging job was when she was an Obituary Writer for the local newspaper. She currently works full time in law enforcement. She graduated with a bachelor's degree in Business Accounting from the University of Phoenix in 2011; and graduated with a master's degree in Business Administration from the University of Phoenix in 2013. In 2016, she received her life insurance license for the State of Louisiana. She currently aspires to become a notary public for Louisiana, an income tax preparer, and to become securities licensed. Her ultimate career goal is to one day become a sole proprietor.

## Candice E. Cox, LCSW

Candice is an author, therapist, public speaker, trainer, and KHAOS Koach! Since 2008 she has provided licensed counseling and consulting families in services to children and various settings. In 2014 she started her nonprofit, KHAOS (Keep Healing And Overcoming Struggles) Inc, and began implementing trauma informed programs in schools and community centers to address the lack of social and emotional coping skills taught both in home and educational environments. She utilizes innovative and experiential treatment modalities to change the focus from people being labeled to living life beyond labels. She believes life happens but it doesn't have to stop. Her goal with every person that She encounter is to help them help themselves as they are the experts of their lives. For these reasons, she loves to be a catalyst in the lives of others to propel them forward.

For more information, visit www.khaosinc.org

## *Ida Jefferson*

Ida Jefferson is a daughter, sister, wife, mother and nurturer. She has worked in different industries for over 50 years. Ida believes that she called to helping God's people to be true to themselves and find the lane to which they belong. She gave her life to Christ at age 13 and has not looked back since.

## **Kimberley Jones, MA**

Kimberley Jones is a wonderful mother, devoted daughter, loving sister, caring aunt and a precious child of God.

Kimberley has been married twice and also celebrated two divorce parties! She possesses both undergraduate and graduate degrees as well as truck driving and nursing licenses. In addition, Kimberley is a proud military veteran.

Kimberley is the mother to a beautiful daughter also named Kimberley whom she loves with ALL her heart.

## Evangelist Kelly L. King, MS MAT

Kelly L. King is a native resident of the Kansas City, Missouri area, where she was born and reared. She was reared in the home with both parents, Leorn and Carol King, 2 siblings, and is the proud mother of 2 children. She received Christ as her Savior at the age of 14, at Sunlight M.B. Church under the teaching and leadership of Founding Pastor, Julius Rambo Sr. and continues to serve in this vineyard under the leadership of Pastor Rickey D. Rambo

Ms. King was educated in the Kansas City, Missouri Schools. She has a Bachelor's of Science in Organizational Leadership with a minor in Biblical Studies and holds a Master's degree in Management from Baker University and a Master's degree in Theological Studies from Midwestern Theological Seminary and Graduate hours toward a Masters in Counseling.

Ms. King teaches Bible Study, the former Bible Instructor for the Sunshine District and General Baptist Convention of Missouri, Kansas and Nebraska Junior Mission Auxiliary. She is the former State President for the General Baptist Convention of MO, KS & NE Women's Intermediate Auxiliary and the District women intermediate Auxiliary President. While in these positions she successfully spearheaded city-wide community events for mentoring and teaching hundreds of young ladies and organized conferences that impacted women from all walks of life. She is a faithful member in varies ministries of the vineyard where she serves. Her volunteer services extend beyond the church and reach the community in such areas of the battered women's shelters and food pantries. She has self-published three books, "Here my prayers O' Lord, Hear my Petitions, Fulfillment, Purpose Destiny, walking in obedience to God and He Makes the difference, living successfully single".

Ms. King often speaks on different programs sharing the gospel of Jesus Christ, along with covering a variety of subjects; conducting seminars, workshops, vacation bible school and other teachings including outreach evangelism and witnessing. She is a mentor to high-school age girls, and an active member of Delta Sigma Theta Sorority Incorporated serving her community.

Ms. King's will is the will of our Lord "For the Son of man is come to seek and to save that which is lost, Luke 19:10. Her desire is to allow God to use her as He has so predestined and purposed.

The biggest and greatest asset in my own words is:
THANK GOD I'M SAVED, therefore, HE CALLS ME FRIEND, HALLELUJAH!

## Queen Leia Lewis

Queen Leia Lewis is a deeply rooted, light working Louisiana woman on a mission to help her Soul Sisters release limiting beliefs, shake off their burdens, and become who they are born to be. As the CEO and creator of Beautiful and Sacred Things, Queen Leia is a masterful Sacred Arts for Living Teacher TM who leads online training, mentoring programs, and healing retreats. She guides growing women to access enduring wisdom,  cultural knowledge, and practical spiritual tools while reawakening the Divine Feminine spirit within. She draws from her rich inner journey and global adventures as a spiritual truth seeker who has traveled to ten countries and counting. Queen Leia is a visionary cultural worker, environmental activist, creative artist, teacher, mother, and healer. She has been celebrated as a presenter and featured speaker for TEDx, Green For All, Maafa New Orleans, and Essence Festival. Visit Queen Leia Lewis' website and discover her complimentary gift for you at www.beautifulandsacredthings.com.

I AM WOMAN: Defining Womanhood And Identity

## Dr. Monique A Maxey

Dr. Monique A. Maxey has served as a strong and viable force within the St. Louis community through activism, mentoring, and volunteering. After twelve years working as a professional within the fields of social service and mental health, she returned to school. She received her doctorate degree in Clinical Psychology with an emphasis in Forensics and Child/Adolescent studies in 2015. Today, she uses writing as a tool toward personal growth and empowerment for herself and for others.

Since beginning her writing career at age six, she has dabbled in several genres of writing, including short stories, scientific journal articles, instructional workbooks, articles, poetry, and fiction. As a spoken word artist, she has performed under stage name Nailah within several local and national venues. She has also hosted her own spoken word event entitled Sistahspeak for five years. Currently, she is authoring a therapeutic children's book to be published later this year.

Monique enjoys serving as a conductor of words both in clinical work and recreational leisure. Her writing weaves character into emotional experiences, social dilemmas, and provides a voice for the voiceless. As a woman with several marginalized identities, Monique resides at the pinnacle of intersectionality, often reflected in her work. A progressive woman who envisions expansion and success for this community, Monique's insight, creativity, and candor help to create the change that our community seeks.

## Dr. Shonta Smith

Shonta M. Smith, Ed.D. is the "Essence of Education". She has defied the odds. From the slums of inner city St. Louis, she knew early on that there was something more. Dr. Smith knew that life in and of itself was great. She knew that greatness was upon her and that it was her responsibility to be true to herself and do great things. Dr. Smith was blessed early on as she had the opportunity to participate in the voluntary desegregation program from 7th thru 12th grade. This experience allowed her to interact with various

cultural groups and develop an appreciation for everyone's cultural uniqueness. This opportunity set the foundation for Dr. Smith's passion on culturally responsive teaching and resulted in the creation of Dr. Shonta Smith International LLC.

Dr. Smith is an Associate Professor in the Department of Elementary, Early and Special Education at Southeast Missouri State University. She has over 24 years of experience in education. Of those 24 years, 17 years have been at the elementary, middle and high school levels. She has been a teacher, team leader, department head, coach, administrative intern and principal with the St. Louis Public Schools, Normandy School District and the Ferguson-Florissant School District. The other 7 years have been at the collegiate level as an Adjunct Professor with Lindenwood University and Associate Professor with Southeast Missouri State University. Her research interests are African Centered Rites of Passage Programs, Culturally Responsive Teaching, and Instructional Leadership. Dr. Smith received her

Ed. D. Doctor of Education in Educational Leadership from St. Louis University, M.Ed. Master of Education in Counseling from the University of Missouri St. Louis and B. S. Bachelor of Science in Education from Harris Stowe State University. She is passionate about educating communities. Her motto is "One Team – One Goal - One Band - One Sound".

## *Vanessa Sutton*

Vanessa Sutton was born and raised in St. Louis, Missouri; attending Forest Park Community and Tarkio Colleges. She is the mother of two children. Vanessa works in I.T. field for over 40 years. She developed a love of poetry and short stories as a youth and has been writing poetry since 1969.

## *Donna Troy*

Donna Troy is an up and coming author. She is currently working on a children's book. Presently working in the field of Human Resources, I live by this motto "if people can accept me at my worst then they will appreciate me at my best". I am small town girl who loves life. Twins run in my family which I am one. Traveling is what I love to do.

## *Dawn Warren*

Dawn Warren has taught English as a Second Language at the elementary level in the Rockwood School District for 17 years. She was historically the first African-American ESOL Teacher in the state of Missouri. Prior to Rockwood, Dawn taught high school Spanish I, II, III & IV and taught adult ESL to migrant workers from Mexico. Dawn received her M.A. in TESOL, B.S. in Spanish and Public Relations and K-12 Certification from the University of Central Missouri. Dawn is currently working on her family's genealogy and plans to write a book in the near future and travel.

## *Wendy Winegardner*

Wendy Winegardner is a first time author, educator, mother of 2 and survivor. In her spare time she likes  to camp, bake, and attend her son's sporting events .She also like to travel to take her daughter to college. Wendy says, "When I grow up, I would like to be a nurse or pastry chef". Currently, she is a second grade teacher in the Rockwood School District.

## The Authoress
## Tonya Wilson

Tonya Wilson aka "Booked On Tonya" is a native of Baltimore, Maryland and spent her early childhood years growing up in a project community known as "Westport". Wilson's love for writing and her life experiences have resulted in her 2015 three part series, "Portrait of a Hustler", "The Chronicles of Toni" and the finale, "Toni Toni Toni" under Polk Publishing House.

Tonya acquired her Bachelor's degree in Mass Communications at Towson State University in 1985. Authoress Wilson is a 2015-2017 featured author with Delta Sigma Theta Sorority, Inc., "Deltas On Tour". In this year 2016, she released "Lipstick Monologues" which is a must read book that she dedicated to all of her Sistahs. She is a contributing author of the 2017 Amazon's Best Seller, "Permission to Win: A Daughter's Guide to Winning From The Inside Out". Tonya was a featured author and award recipient for the 7th Annual African American Exposition. Authoress Wilson is the host and producer of a national Christian based radio broadcast, "Word Up" on W646 Queen City Bullies Radio, North Carolina, and is a motivational speaker with a focus on lifting up and encouraging women.

Tonya is a born again Christian who says it's her duty to share God's love and while her genre of urban fiction writings are unapologetically influenced by her life experiences, controversial issues and shocking hard facts of street life she has

managed to tell her stories with an infusion of spirituality thus sewing unexpected seeds of the "Good News" throughout her writings to an audience that most Churches have either forgotten about or just not taking the extra effort to go after. Wilson says that she is proud to be a ground breaker because no author has stepped out of the box to combine "hardcore" adult urban fiction with a "Christian" message.

# Order Today!

*Great for*
*Grandmothers, Mothers, Sisters, Nieces,*
*Cousins and Friends*
Use
### ***Readbook***
To Get 10% off your next purchase

https://www.paypal.me/cameshacarter

## We want your feedback!!!

Please email me with your questions, comments or praise at camesha@cameshacarter.com.

## We want to speak to your group!

We would love to speak at your conference, women's day events, symposiums, marches, corporate events, sororities and groups! Contact us at:
camesha@cameshacarter.com

## Find us on the web:
www. Cameshacarter.com

## Like Us on Facebook
Dr. Camesha Hill-Carter

## Follow Us On Instagram and Twitter
Instagram: ccamesha
Twitter: CameshaCarter

## Subscribe to our YouTube channel
Dr. Camesha Hill-Carter

I look forward to hearing from you soon!
## Thank You!

www.ingramcontent.com/pod-product-compliance
Lightning Source LLC
Chambersburg PA
CBHW022107160426
43198CB00008B/385